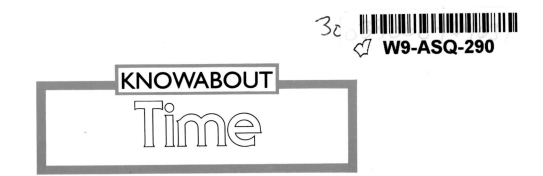

KNOWABOUT
Time

W9-ASQ-290

KNOWABOUT
Time

Text: Henry Pluckrose
Photography: Chris Fairclough

Franklin Watts
London/New York/Sydney/Toronto

© 1988 Franklin Watts

First published in Great Britain by

Franklin Watts
12a Golden Square
London W1

First published in the USA by

Franklin Watts Inc
387 Park Avenue South
New York 10016

ISBN: UK edition 0 86313 509 9

ISBN: US edition 0–531–10452–4
Library of Congress
Catalog Card No: 87–50589

Editor: Ruth Thomson
Design: Edward Kinsey
Additional photographs: Zefa

Typesetting: Keyspools Ltd
Printed in Hong Kong

About this book

This book is designed for use in the home, playgroup and infant school.

Mathematics is part of the child's world. It is not just about interpreting numbers or in mastering the tricks of addition or multiplication. Mathematics is about *Ideas*. These ideas (or concepts) have been developed over the centuries to help explain particular qualities, such as size, weight, height, as well as relationships and comparisons. Yet all too often the important part which an understanding of mathematics will play in a child's development is forgotten or ignored.

Most adults can solve simple mathematical tasks by "doing them in their head." For example you can probably add up or subtract simple numbers without the need for counters, beads or fingers. Young children find such abstractions almost impossible to master. They need to see, talk, touch and experiment.

The photographs in this book and the text which supports them have been prepared with one major aim. They have been chosen to encourage talk around topics which are essentially mathematical. By talking with you, the young reader will be helped to explore some of the central concepts which underpin mathematics. It is upon an understanding of these concepts that a child's future mastery of mathematics will be built.

What time do you get up
in the morning?
How can you tell what time it is?

We tell the time
by using clocks . . .

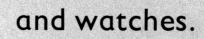
and watches.

We measure short periods of time in seconds.
To time a race a special watch is used which measures in seconds.

The watch is started
when the race starts.
The watch is stopped
when the winner
crosses the finishing line.

Seconds are a very
short amount of time.
How many times
can you clap
in one second?

In ten seconds?

How many letters of the alphabet can you write in ten seconds? In sixty seconds?

We measure longer periods of time
in minutes.
Sixty seconds make a minute.

It takes three minutes to boil an egg.

How long does it take you to have breakfast? Lunch? Supper?

Even longer periods of time
are measured in hours.

The numbers on a clock are the hours.
The little hand points to the hours.
The big hand points to the minutes.

It took an hour to make these cakes.
How many minutes make an hour?

How many hours make a day?
There are twelve hours from mid-day
to midnight.

There are twelve hours from midnight to mid-day.

What things do you do every day?
Do you brush your teeth every day?

Do you feed a pet every day?

How many days
are there
in a week?

What day
is it today?

What day
was it
yesterday?

What day
will it be
tomorrow?

Monday

Tuesday

Wednesday

Thursday

Friday

Saturday

Sunday

What things do you do every week?
Do you go to the library every week?

1	2	3	4	5	6	7
8	9	10	11	12	13	14
15	16	17	18	19	20	21
22	23	24	25	26	27	28
29	30	31				

How many days are there in a month?
What is the date today?

Every month there is a full moon.

January	February	March
April	May	June
July	August	September
October	November	December

Months make up years.

How many months are there in a year?

What month is it now?

When you have a birthday,
what does the number of candles
on your cake mean?

CIA. Nº VUELO	DESTINO	SALIDA	EMBARQUE	PUERTA
				5A
		11.25	11.05	6B
TR.448	IBIZA	12.10	11.50	
IB.024	BARCELONA	13.10	12.50	
AO3240	IBIZA			

SALIDAS NACIONALES →

NACIONAL
RT →

Planes run to a schedule.
To catch a plane,
you need to be at the airport
on time . . .

or the plane will take off without you!

To make toast,
bread has
to be toasted
for the right length
of time . . .

or else you ruin it !

At the end of the day,
it's time for bed.
What time do you go to bed?